I0002684

UNICORN
ACTIVITY BOOK FOR KIDS

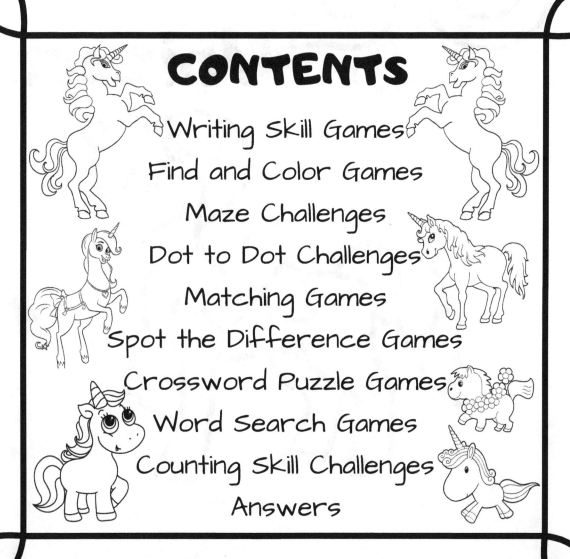

CONTENTS

THIS COLORING BOOK BELONGS TO:

_____

Writing Skill Game:

Uu is for Unicorn

Find and Color Game:

Can you color the unicorn with their assigned color?

1 - pink   3 - red   5 - yellow

2 - violet   4 - orange   6 - blue

Maze Challenge:

Can you help the unicorn to find the way to the castle?

castle

Dot to dots challenge:
Can you connect the dots to create
a charming unicorn?

Matching Test:

Can you encircle the correct unicorn's shadow?

Spot the Difference Game:
Can you find and encircle the difference?

Crossword Puzzle Game:
Can you guess the hidden letters?

Word Search Challenge:

Can you find
the 5 unicorn words?

```
U  L  F  L  P  D  U  U  D  J
N  U  T  D  O  H  N  N  Z  V
I  N  R  T  L  F  I  I  H  Z
C  I  K  B  N  G  C  C  I  U
O  C  E  V  R  O  O  O  E  K
R  O  G  L  T  Z  R  R  E  D
N  R  C  X  Z  A  N  N  H  E
U  N  I  C  O  R  N  G  F  N
M  C  I  L  Q  P  O  X  V  Q
P  Q  Q  X  O  W  V  P  N  E
```

UNICORN   UNICORN   UNICORN
UNICORN   UNICORN

Counting Skills Challenge:

Can you count how many unicorns?

Writing Skill Game: Can you draw the capital letter U?

Writing Skill Game: Can you draw the small letter U?

Writing Skill Game:

Can you help the unicorn to get the sweets?

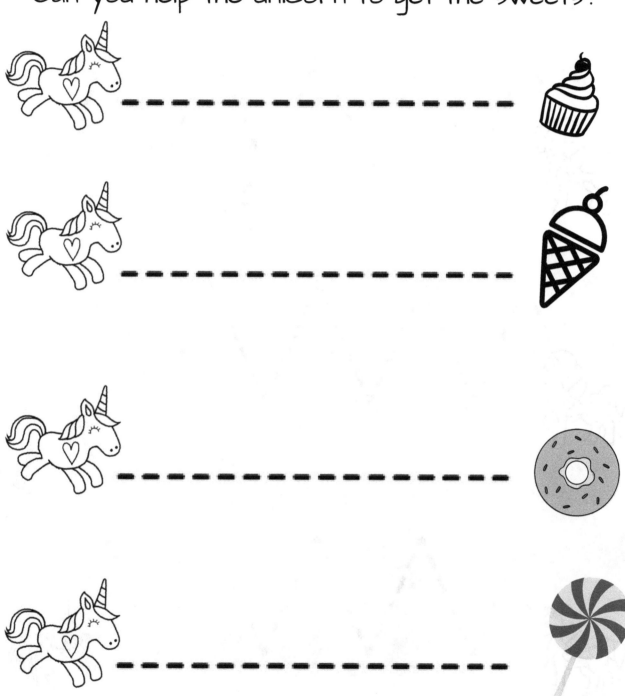

Writing Skill Game:

Can you help the unicorn to find the way to her friends?

Writing Skill Game:

Can you help the unicorn to find the way to the castle?

Writing Skill Game:

Can you help the baby unicorns tracing
the lines to create shapes?

Writing Skill Game:

Can you guess the correct hidden letters?

| U | | I | | O | | N |

| S | | | A | | R |

| | O | | O | |

| C | | O | | D |

| R | | I | | B | | W |

Writing Skill Game:

Can you guess the correct hidden letters?

| U | | I | | O | | N |

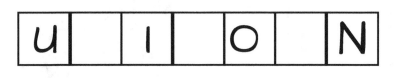

| C | | P | | A | | E |

| C | | K | |

| D | | N | | T |

| I | | E | | R | | A | |

Writing Skill Game:

Can you guess the correct hidden letters?

U | I | O | N

M | R | A | D

F | I | Y

D | A | O

P | I | C | S

Find and Color Game:

Which one is the unicorn?

Find and Color Game:
Can you color the unicorn with their assigned color?

1 - red   3 - yellow   5 - blue   7 - pink

2 - orange 4 - green   6 - violet 8 - white

Find and Color Game:
Where is the unicorn?

Find and Color Game:

Which one is the unicorn?

Find and Color Game:
Can you color the unicorn with their assigned color?

1 - violet

2 - pink

3 - yellow

4 - orange

5 - red

6 - blue

Find and Color Game:

Where are the 2 unicorns?

Find and Color Game:
Can you color the unicorn with their assigned color?

1 - pink   3 - yellow   5 - blue

2 - violet   4 - orange   6 - red

Find and Color Game:

Which one is the unicorn?

Find and Color Game:

Where are the 3 unicorns?

Maze Challenge:
Which path should the unicorn take way to her friends?

Maze Challenge:
Can you help the unicorn to get the ice cream?

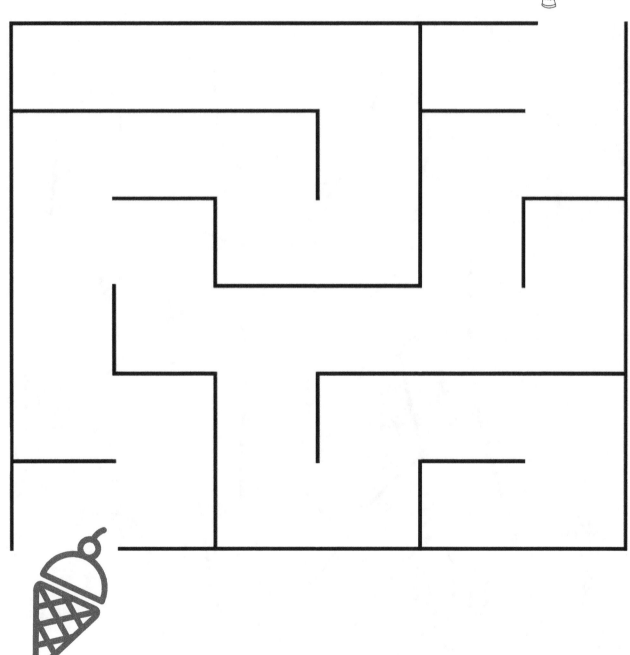

Maze Challenge:

Can you help the unicorn to get the cupcake?

Maze Challenge:

Can you help the unicorn and the fairy to find their way to the magic land?

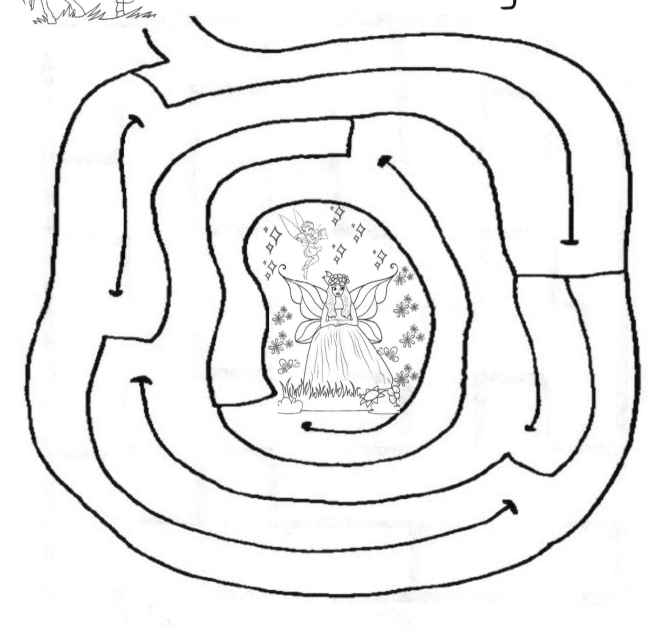

Maze Challenge: Can you help the flying
unicorn and her friends
to get the magic wand?

Maze Challenge:

Can you help the unicorn to get the cake?

Maze Challenge:

Can you guide the unicorn to get the gift?

Maze Challenge: Can you help the the unicorn to find the way to the rainbow clouds?

Maze Challenge:

Can you help the unicorn
to save the princess?

Dot to dots challenge:

Can you connect the dots to create a cute unicorn?

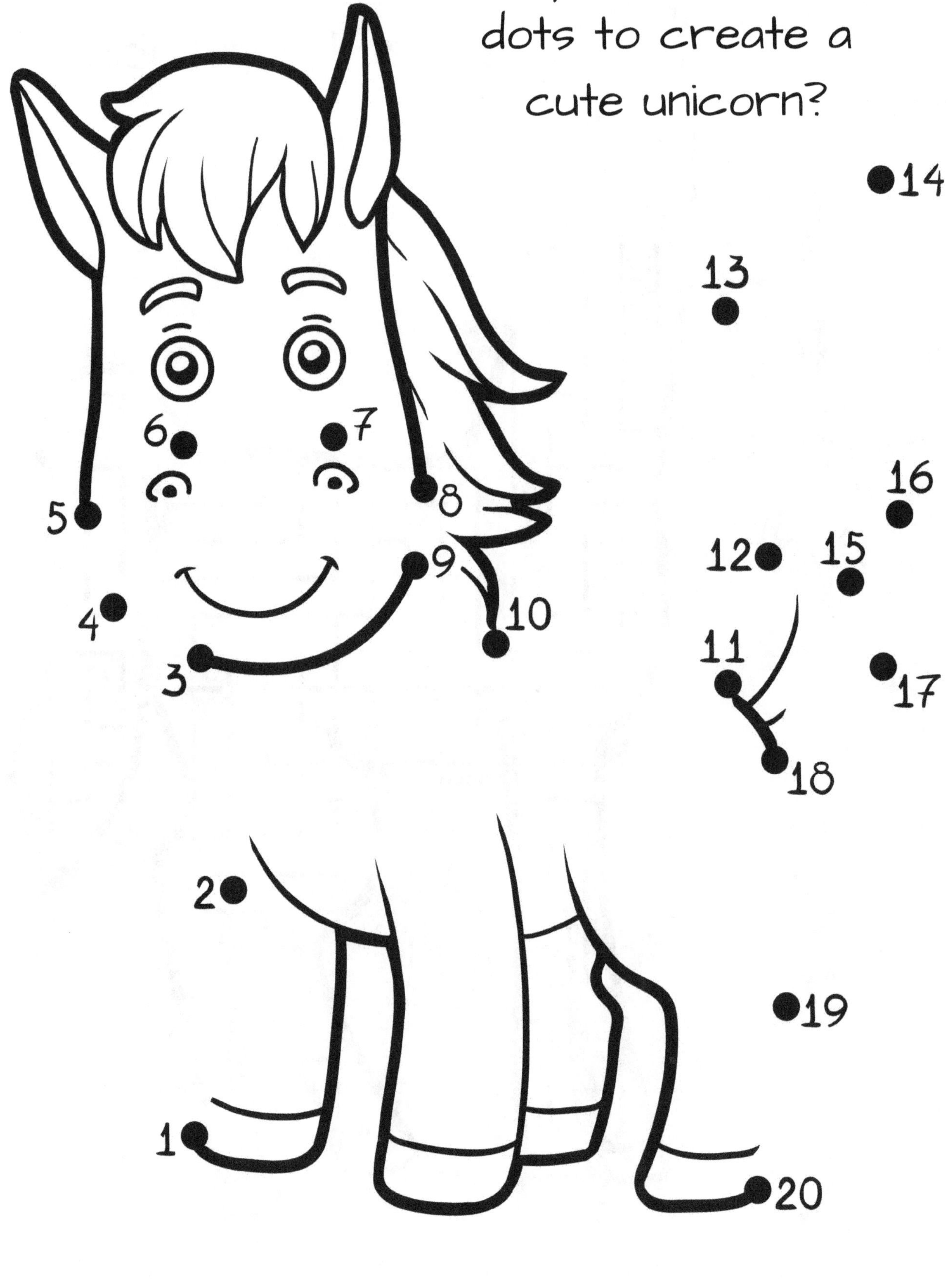

● 14

13
●

● 6   7 ●

5 ●   8 ●

16
●

12 ●   15 ●

9 ●   11 ●   17 ●

4 ●   10 ●

3 ●   18

2 ●

● 19

1 ●   ● 20

Dot to dots challenge:
Can you connect the dots to create
an adorable unicorn?

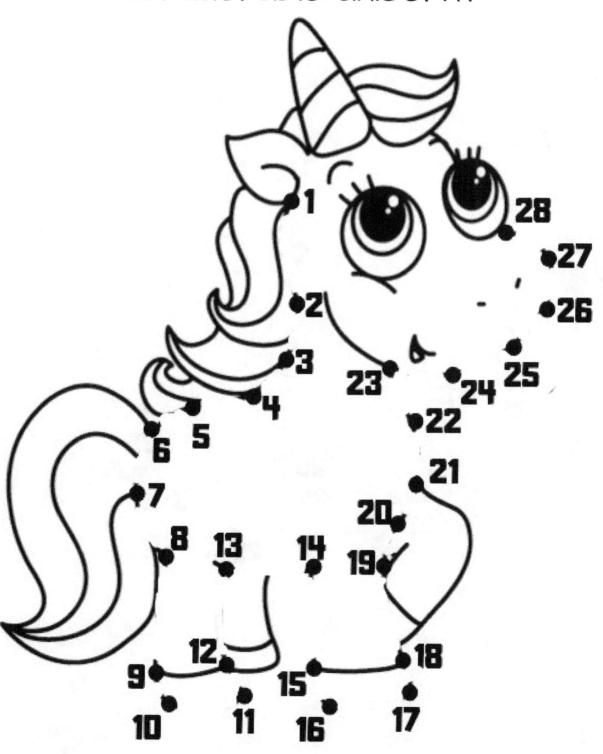

Dot to dots challenge:
Can you connect the dots to create
a pretty unicorn?

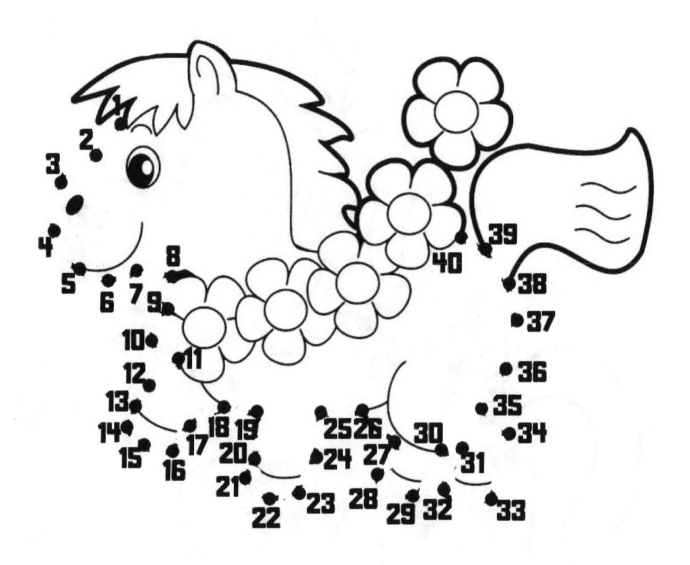

Dot to dots challenge:
Can you connect the dots to create
a flying unicorn?

Dot to dots challenge:

Can you connect the dots to create
a lovely unicorn?

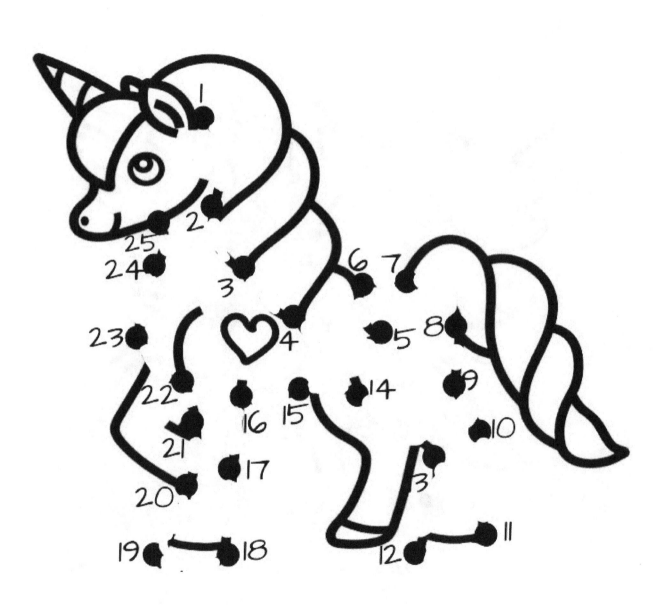

Dot to dots challenge:
Can you connect the dots to create a gorgeous unicorn?

Dot to dots challenge:
Can you connect
the dots to create
a magical unicorn?

32

33

31 30

34 29

28
27

23
24 26
25

22

35

21

20 19

10 18

36

11

17

8 9

13 12 16
15

37

14

7

38

6

39

5

4

3

2

1

Dot to dots challenge:

Can you connect the dots to create a fascinating unicorn?

Dot to dots challenge:
Can you connect the dots to create a charming unicorn?

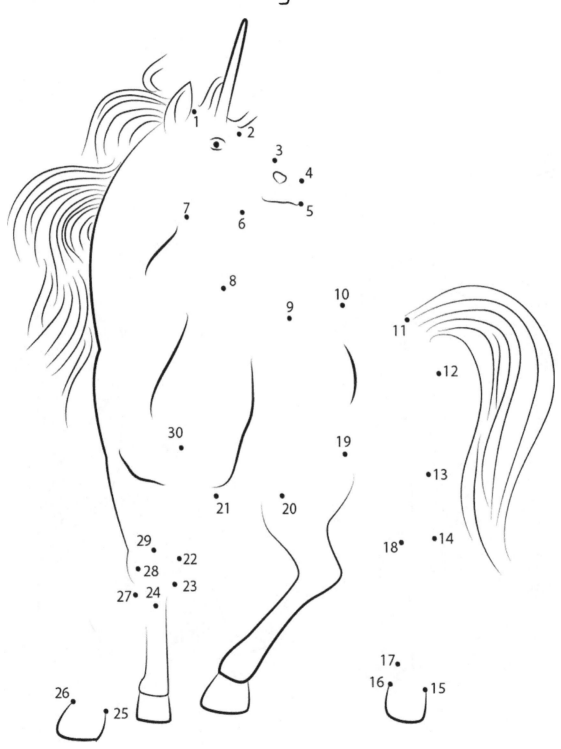

Matching Test:

Can you draw a line from each picture to the matching word?

moon

rainbow

unicorn

heart

star

Matching Test:
Can you draw a line to match the correct unicorn's shadow?

Matching Test:

Can you draw a line from each picture to the matching word?

cupcake

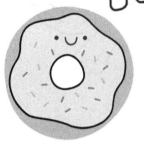

cake

unicorn

donut

ice cream

Matching Test:
Can you encircle which two baby unicorns are twins?

Matching Test:

Can you draw a line from each picture to the matching word?

dragon

unicorn

dinosaur

Matching Test:
Can you encircle the 3 matching unicorns ?

Let's party!

Matching Test:

Can you draw a line to match the unicorn parents to their children?

Matching Test:

Can you encircle the two unicorns that are exactly the same?

Matching Test:

Can you draw a line from each picture to the matching word?

mermaid

princess

unicorn

fairy

Spot the Difference Game:
Which one is different from the others?

Spot the Difference Game:

Can you spot the
2 differences
between the
pictures?

Spot the Difference Game:

Which one is different from the others?

Spot the Difference Game:

Can you find and encircle the 3 differences between the pictures?

Spot the Difference Game:

Which one is different from the others?

Spot the Difference Game:

Can you spot the 4 differences ?

Spot the Difference Game:

Which one is different from the others?

Spot the Difference Game:

Can you encircle the 5 differences?

Spot the Difference Game:

Which one is different from the others?

Crossword Puzzle Game:
Can you guess the hidden letters?

Crossword Puzzle Game:
Can you guess the hidden letters?

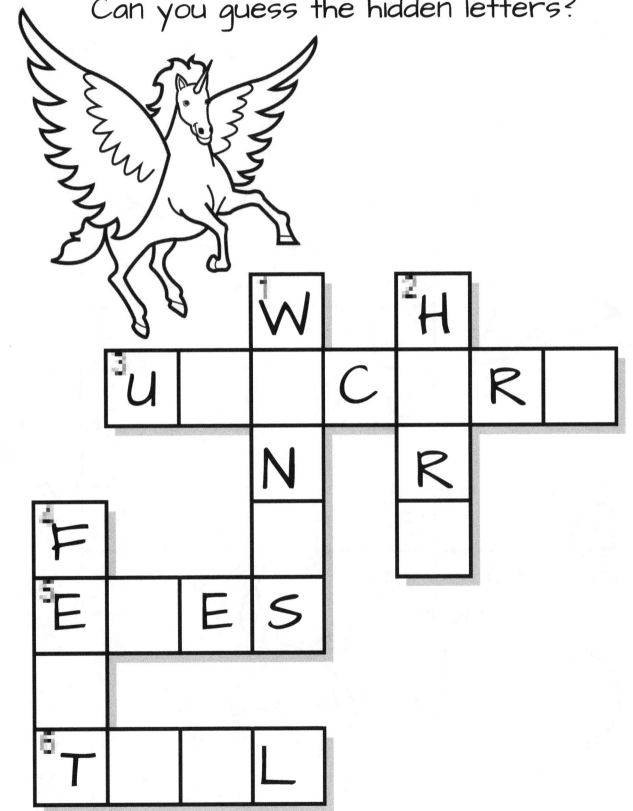

Crossword Puzzle Game:
Can you guess the hidden letters?

Crossword Puzzle Game:

Can you guess the
hidden letters?

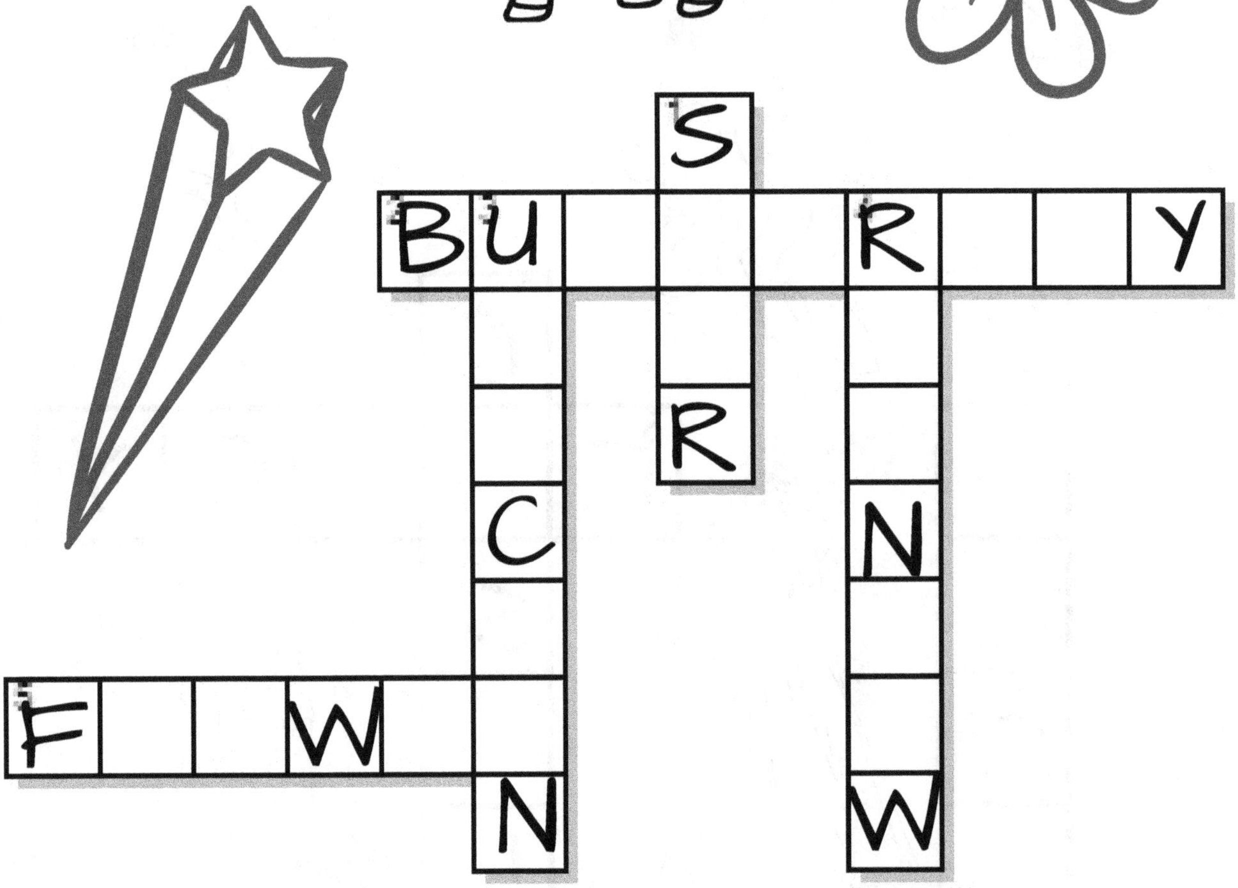

B U   S   R   Y

R

C

F   W

N   N

W

Crossword Puzzle Game:

Can you guess the hidden letters?

Crossword Puzzle Game:
Can you guess the hidden letters?

U

C

F

Y

M R M

P R N

C

E

Crossword Puzzle Game:

Can you guess the hidden letters?

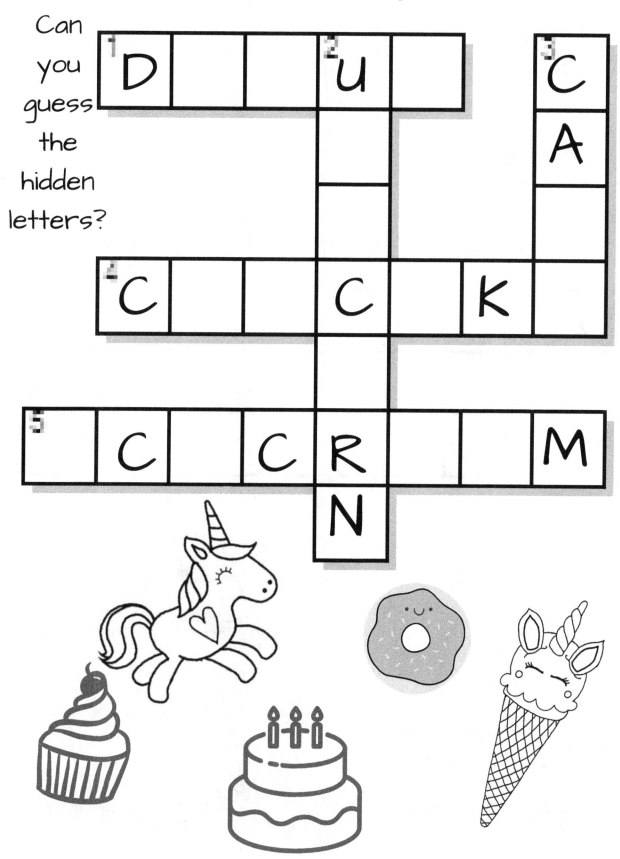

Crossword Puzzle Game:

Can you guess the hidden letters?

U

D

D

Crossword Puzzle Game:
Can you guess the hidden letters?

Word Search Challenge:

Can you look for the 6 magical words?

```
F  P  W  J  K  C  A  U  P  H
G  F  Q  R  S  B  Z  N  M  X
W  N  X  K  T  N  K  I  O  B
B  C  X  X  A  G  R  C  O  D
Y  L  Z  E  R  A  G  O  N  I
G  O  G  N  N  E  K  R  D  V
D  U  U  L  W  S  U  N  T  S
I  D  D  S  H  L  K  Q  C  X
R  A  I  N  B  O  W  D  A  W
C  P  H  Z  R  G  E  R  I  S
```

UNICORN	CLOUD	RAINBOW
STAR	SUN	MOON

Word Search Challenge:

Can you search for the 6 words?

```
S  B  C  A  W  I  P  G  S  E
T  U  J  C  Y  X  D  G  H  K
F  T  U  V  F  G  R  M  D  I
A  T  N  O  L  G  A  A  K  E
I  E  I  A  O  N  G  G  B  P
R  R  C  N  W  M  O  I  C  N
Y  F  O  H  E  A  N  C  A  U
D  L  R  W  R  V  F  E  A  Z
W  Y  N  E  N  U  L  O  S  W
P  D  D  A  E  Z  Y  Y  N  R
```

UNICORN   FAIRY   BUTTERFLY

DRAGONFLY FLOWER   MAGIC

Word Search Challenge:

Can you find the 6 magical creature words?

```
G  A  K  F  T  Q  Y  U  T  J
D  Y  C  P  P  C  H  N  Y  Q
R  S  M  E  R  M  A  I  D  P
A  M  F  T  I  T  R  C  Y  Y
G  Y  A  H  N  Q  C  O  G  Z
O  X  I  R  C  T  A  R  Z  Q
N  J  R  E  E  N  S  N  P  P
V  R  Y  F  S  X  T  R  B  U
U  X  K  U  S  S  L  Q  E  I
W  R  Y  P  E  F  E  S  M  E
```

UNICORN	MERMAID	PRINCESS
FAIRY	CASTLE	DRAGON

Word Search Challenge:

Can you look for the 7 animal words?

```
F  P  U  N  I  C  O  R  N  R
S  P  L  K  E  O  J  T  F  H
H  J  M  L  L  X  N  U  Z  I
G  U  G  P  E  L  K  R  A  N
V  Y  I  B  P  I  G  I  V  O
W  J  R  Z  H  O  J  N  V  C
B  R  A  E  A  N  W  G  W  E
F  Q  F  B  N  A  Q  I  M  R
L  E  F  R  T  I  G  E  R  O
Q  I  E  A  Q  R  C  K  Z  S
```

UNICORN   GIRAFFE   ZEBRA
ELEPHANT   RHINOCEROS LION
TIGER

Word Search Challenge:

Can you look for the 7 delicious words?

```
M H N W C I W S Q D
D C Z X M O Z D Q O
C A C I T R D D I N
U K Q I I U G Q N U
P E J C R E A M O T
C M P E A C U Y D L
A G Q S I G M S H S
K X D P I Z Z A B U
E Z G Y O C Y T X K
U N I C O R N Q N U
```

UNICORN   DONUT   ICE

CREAM   CAKE   PIZZA

CUPCAKE

Word Search Challenge:

Can you search for the
unicorn's part of the body?

```
O  D  W  I  N  G  S  W  M  Q
J  J  J  E  O  L  O  A  O  S
O  Z  F  E  E  T  M  V  A  R
Y  Q  F  V  F  F  L  M  P  V
T  A  I  L  E  Y  E  S  C  H
G  T  M  N  N  N  K  H  E  F
V  H  O  S  G  E  U  O  F  R
N  J  U  N  I  C  O  R  N  P
V  S  T  P  Z  K  F  N  N  X
Q  I  H  X  W  E  S  N  U  Y
```

UNICORN	HORN	WINGS
TAIL	EYES	FEET
MOUTH	NECK	

Word Search Challenge:

Can you find the 7 different shapes?

```
D  N  W  S  X  N  P  H  N  R
Q  R  T  Q  V  N  L  Z  S  E
Z  A  P  U  S  X  K  S  Q  C
U  D  I  A  M  O  N  D  A  T
N  J  N  R  T  V  R  W  Z  A
I  R  T  E  E  H  Z  Y  G  N
C  I  R  C  L  E  B  U  Z  G
O  B  D  A  R  A  M  S  Q  L
R  S  S  T  A  R  Q  Z  I  E
N  J  Z  G  R  T  P  B  X  C
```

UNICORN   STAR   HEART
CIRCLE   SQUARE   DIAMOND
RECTANGLE

Word Search Challenge:

Can you search for the 5 magical creatures?

```
P  B  F  A  I  R  Y  Z  E  N
E  S  D  B  Y  R  Y  L  S  O
S  U  X  C  I  K  T  U  O  G
O  S  S  J  L  S  J  Q  C  A
H  S  E  V  A  U  I  X  B  R
U  N  I  C  O  R  N  U  F  D
A  Z  X  F  N  W  R  W  R  G
X  I  X  R  I  I  I  G  S  B
L  I  G  F  Z  T  R  W  Z  J
Y  N  N  F  L  G  L  P  P  X
```

UNICORN   PRINCESS   FAIRY

DRAGON   CASTLE

Word Search Challenge:

Can you search for the 6 creatures?

```
Y D R A G O N F L Y
J M E R M A I D X U
Z H U M R G F D Y V
T C G E F Q E C P Q
N F K Z R P Y Y B L
M V B K F V Z C U D
R U A S O N I D J R
U N I C O R N K H E
S O R E C O N I H R
Q P E G A S U S P G
```

UNICORN   DINOSAUR   DRAGONFLY
RHINOCEROS MERMAID   PEGASUS

Counting Skills Challenge:

How many unicorns are there?

Counting Skills Challenge:

Can you count how many baby unicorns are there?

Counting Skills Challenge:

How many unicorns are there?

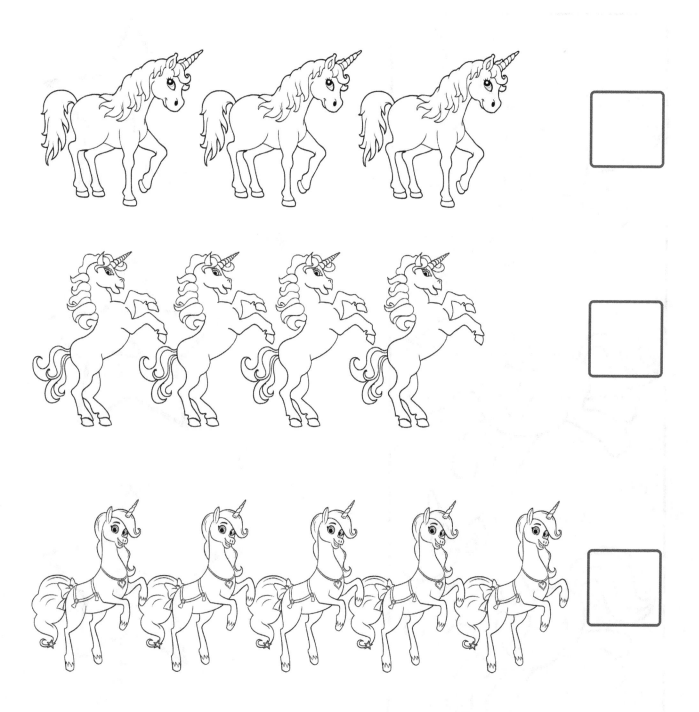

Counting Skills Challenge:

Can you color the star of the correct count?

Counting Skills Challenge:

Can you color the cloud of the correct count?

Counting Skills Challenge:

Can you draw a line to the star of the correct corresponding count?

Counting Skills Challenge:

Can you draw a line to the cloud of the correct corresponding count?

Counting Skills Challenge:

Can you write inside the star the correct count
of the flying baby unicorns?

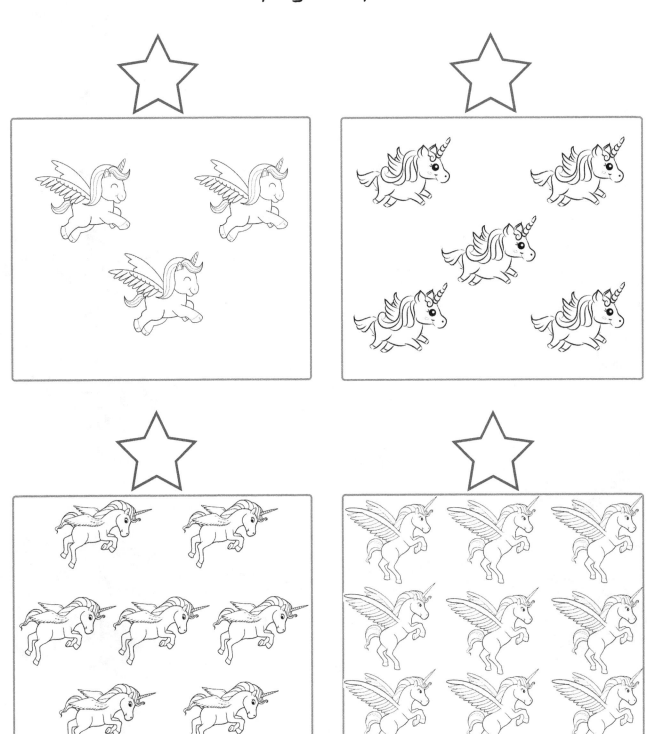

Counting Skills Challenge:

Can you write inside the cloud the correct count
of the flying unicorns?

Answers

Writing Skill Game:

Uu is for **Unicorn**

U U U U U
u u u u u u

Find and Color Game:
Can you color the unicorn with their assigned color?

1 - pink   3 - red   5 - yellow
2 - violet   4 - orange   6 - blue

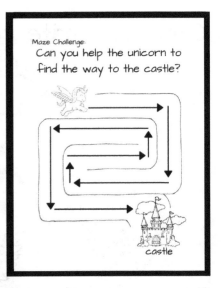

Maze Challenge:
Can you help the unicorn to find the way to the castle?

castle

Dot to dots challenge:
Can you connect the dots to create a charming unicorn?

Matching Test:
Can you encircle the correct unicorn's shadow?

Spot the Difference Game:
Can you find and encircle the difference?

Crossword Puzzle Game:
Can you guess the hidden letters?

MOON
STAR
RAINBOW
UNICORN
CLOUD

Word Search Challenge:
Can you find the 5 unicorn words?

UNICORN   UNICORN   UNICORN
UNICORN   UNICORN

Counting Skills Challenge:
Can you count how many unicorns?

3

Answers for Writing Skill Games

Writing Skill Game: Can you draw the capital letter U?

U U U U U
U U U U U
U U U U U
U U U U U
U U U U U

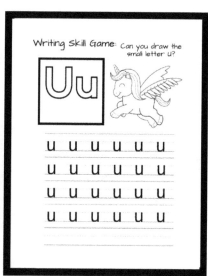

Writing Skill Game: Can you draw the small letter u?

u u u u u u
u u u u u u
u u u u u u
u u u u u u

Writing Skill Game:

Can you help the unicorn to get the sweets?

Writing Skill Game:

Can you help the unicorn to find the way to her friends?

Writing Skill Game:

Can you help the unicorn to find the way to the castle?

Writing Skill Game:

Can you help the baby unicorns tracing the lines to create shapes?

Writing Skill Game:

Can you guess the correct hidden letters?

UNICORN
STAR
MOON
CLOUD
RAINBOW

Writing Skill Game:

Can you guess the correct hidden letters?

UNICORN
CUPCAKE
CAKE
DONUT
ICECREAM

Writing Skill Game:

Can you guess the correct hidden letters?

UNICORN
MERMAID
FAIRY
DRAGON
PRINCESS

Answers for Find and Color Games

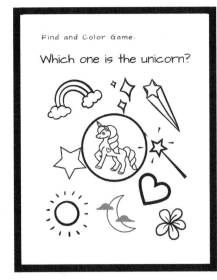

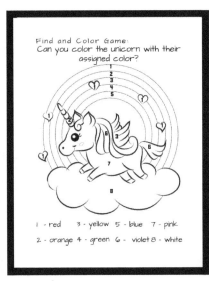

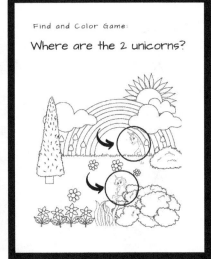

Answers for Mazes Challenges

Maze Challenge:
Which path should the unicorn take way to her friends?

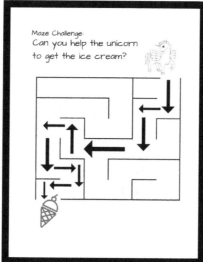

Maze Challenge:
Can you help the unicorn to get the ice cream?

Maze Challenge:
Can you help the unicorn to get the cupcake?

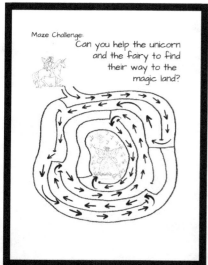

Maze Challenge:
Can you help the unicorn and the fairy to find their way to the magic land?

Maze Challenge: Can you help the flying unicorn and her friends to get the magic wand?

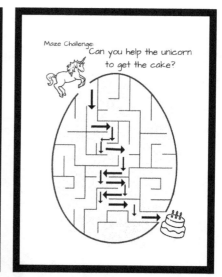

Maze Challenge:
Can you help the unicorn to get the cake?

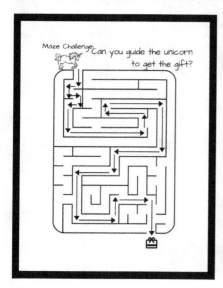

Maze Challenge: Can you guide the unicorn to get the gift?

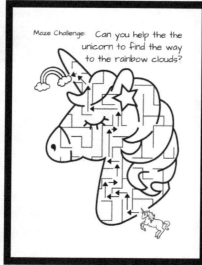

Maze Challenge: Can you help the the unicorn to find the way to the rainbow clouds?

Maze Challenge:
Can you help the unicorn to save the princess?

Answers for Dot to Dot Challenges

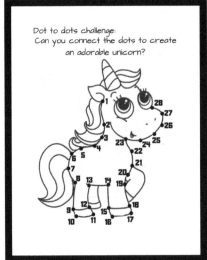

Answers for Matching Games

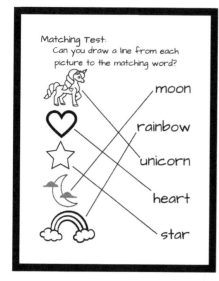

Matching Test:
   Can you draw a line from each picture to the matching word?

moon
rainbow
unicorn
heart
star

Matching Test:
   Can you draw a line to match the correct unicorn's shadow?

Matching Test:
   Can you draw a line from each picture to the matching word?

cupcake
cake
unicorn
donut
ice cream

Matching Test:
   Can you encircle which two baby unicorns are twins?

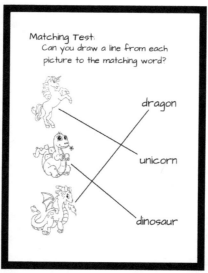

Matching Test:
   Can you draw a line from each picture to the matching word?

dragon
unicorn
dinosaur

Matching Test:
   Can you encircle the 3 matching unicorns?

Let's party!

Matching Test:
   Can you draw a line to match the unicorn parents to their children?

Matching Test:
   Can you encircle the two unicorns that are exactly the same?

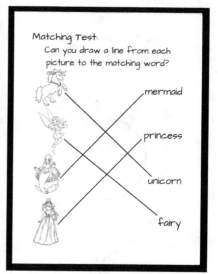

Matching Test:
   Can you draw a line from each picture to the matching word?

mermaid
princess
unicorn
fairy

Answers for Spot the Difference GAmes

Spot the Difference Game:
Which one is different from the others?

Spot the Difference Game:
Can you spot the 2 differences between the pictures?

Spot the Difference Game:
Which one is different from the others?

Spot the Difference Game:
Can you find and encircle the 3 differences between the pictures?

Spot the Difference Game:
Which one is different from the others?

Spot the Difference Game:
Can you spot the 4 differences?

Spot the Difference Game:
Which one is different from the others?

Spot the Difference Game:
Can you encircle the 5 differences?

Spot the Difference Game:
Which one is different from the others?

Answers for Crossword Puzzle

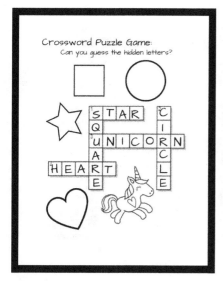

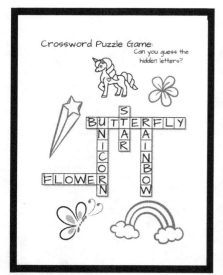

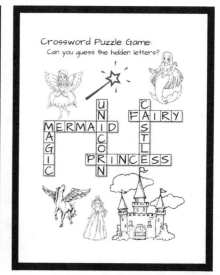

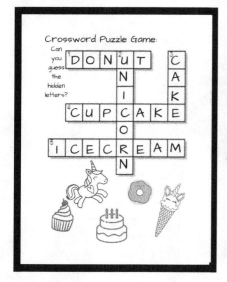

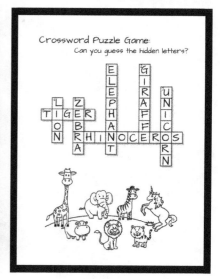

Answers for Word Search Games

Word Search Challenge:
Can you look for the 6 magical words?

F	P	W	J	K	C	A	U	P	H
G	F	Q	R	S	B	Z	N	M	X
W	N	X	K	T	N	K	I	O	O
B	C	X	X	A	G	R	C	O	O
Y	L	Z	E	R	A	G	O	N	V
G	O	G	N	N	E	K	R	D	V
D	U	U	L	W	S	U	N	T	S
I	D	D	S	H	L	K	Q	C	X
R	A	I	N	B	O	W	D	A	W
C	P	H	Z	R	G	E	R	I	S

UNICORN CLOUD RAINBOW
STAR SUN MOON

Word Search Challenge:
Can you search for the 6 words?

UNICORN FAIRY BUTTERFLY
DRAGONFLY FLOWER MAGIC

Word Search Challenge:
Can you find the 6 magical creature words?

UNICORN MERMAID PRINCESS
FAIRY CASTLE DRAGON

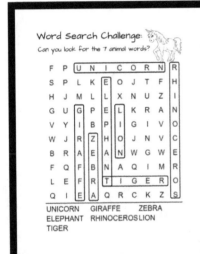

Word Search Challenge:
Can you look for the 7 animal words?

UNICORN GIRAFFE ZEBRA
ELEPHANT RHINOCEROS LION
TIGER

Word Search Challenge:
Can you look for the 7 delicious words?

UNICORN DONUT ICE
CREAM CAKE PIZZA
CUPCAKE

Word Search Challenge:
Can you search for the unicorn's part of the body?

UNICORN HORN WINGS
TAIL EYES FEET
MOUTH NECK

Word Search Challenge:
Can you find the 7 different shapes?

UNICORN STAR HEART
CIRCLE SQUARE DIAMOND
RECTANGLE

Word Search Challenge:
Can you search for the 5 magical creatures?

UNICORN PRINCESS FAIRY
DRAGON CASTLE

Word Search Challenge:
Can you search for the 6 creatures?

UNICORN DINOSAUR DRAGONFLY
RHINOCEROS MERMAID PEGASUS

Answers for Counting Skill Challenges

Counting Skills Challenge:
How many unicorns are there?

4

Counting Skills Challenge:
Can you count how many baby unicorns are there?

2

3

4

Counting Skills Challenge:
How many unicorns are there?

3

4

5

Counting Skills Challenge:
Can you color the star of the correct count?

1

2

3

Counting Skills Challenge:
Can you color the cloud of the correct count?

3

4

5

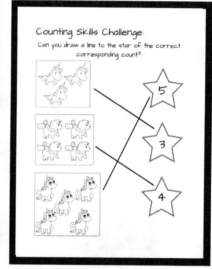

Counting Skills Challenge:
Can you draw a line to the star of the correct corresponding count?

5

3

4

Counting Skills Challenge:
Can you draw a line to the cloud of the correct corresponding count?

6

4

8

10

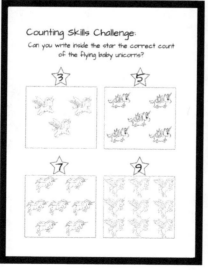

Counting Skills Challenge:
Can you write inside the star the correct count of the flying baby unicorns?

3

5

7

9

Counting Skills Challenge:
Can you write inside the cloud the correct count of the flying unicorns?

4

6

8

9

www.ingramcontent.com/pod-product-compliance
Lightning Source LLC
Chambersburg PA
CBHW080558060326
40689CB00021B/4891